Greek Americans

TIFFANY PETERSON

Heinemann Library
Chicago, Illinois

Designed by Roslyn Broder
Photo research by Scott Braut
Printed in China by WKT Company Limited

08 07 06 05 04
10 9 8 7 6 5 4 3 2 1

Library of Congress Cataloging-in-Publication Data
Peterson, Tiffany.
 Greek Americans / Tiffany Peterson.
    p. cm. -- (We are America)
 Summary: An overview of the history and daily lives of Greek people who immigrated to the United States.
 Includes bibliographical references (p.) and index.
 ISBN 1-4034-5021-8
 1. Greek Americans--History--Juvenile literature. 2. Greek Americans--Social life and customs--Juvenile literature. [1. Greek Americans.] I. Title. II. Series.
 E184.G7P475 2004
 973'.0489--dc22
                         2003021701

Acknowledgments
The author and publisher are grateful to the following for permission to reproduce copyright material: pp. 4, 5, 28, 29 Courtesy of Dr. Nicholas Kefalides; pp. 7, 17, 18, 19, 26 Library of Congress; pp. 8, 11, 16, 20 Courtesy of the Hellenic Museum and Cultural Center, Chicago, Illinois; p. 9 Corbis; pp. 10, 12, 13 Bettmann/Corbis; p. 14 Immigration History Research Center/University of Minnesota; p. 21 Jill Birschbach/Heinemann Library; p. 22 Frances M. Roberts; p. 23 Tony Freeman/Photo Edit; p. 24 Michael Newman/Photo Edit; p. 25 Nancy Sheehan/Photo Edit; p. 27 Reuters NewMedia Inc./Corbis

Cover photographs courtesy of Dr. Nicholas Kefalides, (background) Jill Birschbach/Heinemann Library

The author wishes to thank the following people for all of their help: Dr. Nicholas Kefalides, Dr. Paul Kefalides, and Brian Krumm. Special thanks to Elaine Thomopoulos, Ph.D., cochairman of the Oral History Committee of the Hellenic Museum and Cultural Center, Chicago, and co–project director of the Greeks of Berrien County, Michigan historical association project, for her comments made in preparation of this book.

Some quotations and material used in this book come from the following sources. In some cases, quotes have been abridged or edited for clarity: pp. 9, 13, 15 *Ellis Island Interviews: In Their Own Words* by Peter Morton Coan (New York: Facts on File, 1998); pp. 10, 21 *They Chose America: Conversations with Immigrants* (Princeton, N.J.: Visual Education Corp., 1975).

For more information on the people on the cover of this book, turn to page 29. A present-day photo of the Greektown neighborhood in Chicago is shown in the background.

Contents

Some words are shown in bold, **like this.** You can find out what they mean by looking in the glossary.

To America!

Nicholas Kefalides grew up in Greece. He worked hard in school and enjoyed exploring caves, reading, and listening to music. When he was a teenager, Greece was attacked by Germany. From 1941 to 1944, Greece was controlled by the German government. The German police, known as the Gestapo, arrested Nicholas and his brother. The brothers were part of a group that secretly worked to defeat the German army during **World War Two.** The Gestapo sent the brothers to a **concentration camp** for two months. After he was released, Nicholas finished high school.

This photo of Nicholas was taken in Athens, Greece, in May 1947, the month he sailed for the United States.

Nicholas wanted to be a doctor. After high school, he started medical school in Greece. He decided to finish school in the United States. He had an uncle who was a doctor in Chicago, Illinois.

This uncle helped him come to the U.S. In 1947, Nicholas boarded a ship named the *Saturnia*. He traveled for two weeks across the Atlantic Ocean to New York.

This photo of the Kefalides family was taken in Thessaloníki, Greece, in 1947.

Greece

Greece is a small country in southern Europe. It is made up of a **mainland** and hundreds of islands. Two seas border the mainland— the Ionian on the west and the Aegean on the east. The land in Greece is very rocky. Many mountains divide the country. Today, about ten and a half million people live in Greece.

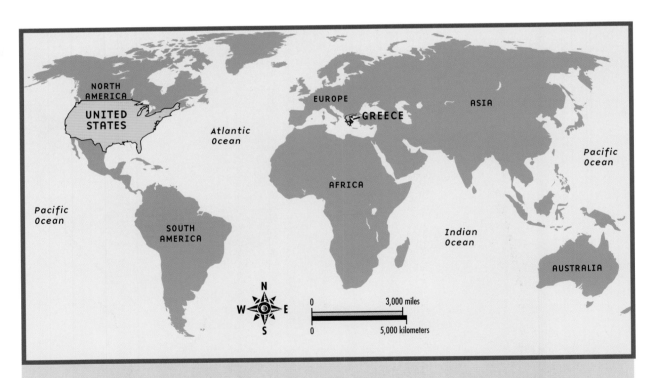

In Greece, the sea is never more than 85 miles (137 kilometers) away no matter where you are in the country. This map shows where Greece and the United States are located in the world.

These children are shown in Athens, Greece, in November 1918. The child on the left is carrying his homework. The other two are working as a delivery boy and as a water carrier.

In the late 1800s, Greek people started leaving their homeland because they could not make enough money to live. Some Greeks wanted to leave their country because of unfair leaders. One ruler made farmers pay high taxes. The taxes made it very difficult for farmers to make money by farming the land. Some farmers saw coming to the United States as a chance for a new beginning.

The first Olympic Games were held in Athens, Greece, more than 2,500 years ago.

Early Greek Immigrants

In 1528, a Greek man named Theodoros came to what is now Florida. He was traveling with a group of Spanish explorers. He was the first Greek person to come to North America. After Theodoros, very few Greeks came to the United States until 1900. From 1900 to 1930, however, about half a million Greeks came to the U.S.

While I was going to school, I always used to tell my friends, "I'm going to America. There is no progress here. What you are, you . . . remain the same way . . . There weren't dreams to develop. The rich people remain rich. The poor people remain poor."

—Doukenie Papandreos, who immigrated in 1919 when she was 15 years old

These Greek girls came to Chicago with their families in the early 1900s.

8

Time Line

1900–1920 About 351,720 Greeks immigrate to the United States.

1924 The U.S. limits the number of immigrants coming into the country each year. Only 307 Greek immigrants were allowed each year.

1946–1960 About 56,000 Greek people who were left homeless after **World War Two** and a **civil war** come to the U.S.

1967–1974 More than 100,000 Greeks immigrate to the U.S. to get away from a group of cruel rulers called "the colonels" in Greece.

Most Greek **immigrants** in the early 1900s were farmers. During the 1890s, many farmers in Greece grew **currants.** Currant prices suddenly dropped, however. Farmers could not make enough money selling them. Many other Greek people had a hard time making money because of high taxes they had to pay the government. Greek people began to move to the U.S. because they thought they could make and save more money there.

These Greek farmers were photographed in Greece in 1906.

Making the Journey

In the late 1890s and early 1900s, Greek farmers sometimes sold their land and animals in order to pay for the trip to the United States. Most often, however, they sold only what they had to, because they planned to return to Greece after making money. Most early Greek **immigrants** were men. Those who had money often spent all of it on the journey. Sometimes, a family member or friend in the U.S. would send the money needed for the trip.

> [It] was awful. Because of the rough sea, the boat couldn't go ahead. In fact, it was four or five days that we were going backward instead of forward.
>
> —Sam Fortosis, who immigrated from Greece in 1914

These Greek women are shown aboard a ship in 1921 on their way to the U.S.

Many Greek immigrants started families after they arrived in the United States. This photo shows three Greek-American families in Chicago.

Before 1907, immigrants first had to travel to a Greek **port** city. From there, they traveled to another port in Europe. The entire trip from Greece to the United States could take as long as 30 days. Most Greek immigrants did not have a lot

Beginning in 1907, Greek immigrants could take a ship from Piraeus, Greece, directly to New York City.

of money. So they usually traveled in **steerage** class. They slept in the bottom of the ship where bunk beds were stacked three high. It was crowded and dirty.

Arriving in the United States

Most of the ships carrying **immigrants** landed in New York. Immigrants traveling in **steerage** class were taken on smaller boats to the Ellis Island Immigration Station. There, they were asked questions about their plans. There were so many people at Ellis Island that sometimes immigrants had to wait days to get through this interview process.

This Greek family arrived at Ellis Island in 1925.

These Greek immigrants are shown at Ellis Island in the 1920s.

I saw the Statue of Liberty. And I said to myself, "Lady, you're beautiful. You opened your arms. Give me a chance to prove that I am worth it, to do something, to become somebody in America." And always, while I was here, that statue was in my mind.

—Doukenie Papandreos, who immigrated in 1919 when she was 15

Immigrants also had to pass health exams. People who were healthy were allowed to go into New York City and on to their final destination. Those who were sick were usually kept in **quarantine.** Those who were very sick were usually cared for in a hospital or sent back to Greece.

Life in the United States

Even though most Greek **immigrants** had been farmers in Greece, they generally moved to cities in the United States. For many, the farming experience in Greece had not been good. They had not been able to make much money at farming. Memories of being hungry were too clear.

*These Greek-American women are shown wearing **traditional** Greek costumes in St. Louis, Missouri, in the 1930s.*

Greek Immigration to the United States

This map shows some of the cities and states that Greek people first came to in the U.S. and where many Greek Americans live today.

In 1920, New York, Chicago, San Francisco, Detroit, and Lowell, Massachusetts, had the largest Greek immigrant populations. When they first came to the U.S., most Greek immigrants did not speak English. It was important to them to be near others who spoke Greek. The areas where Greeks lived together became known as Greektowns. They were like small Greek villages in the U.S.

We first settled on the Lower West Side of Manhattan [in New York City], 22nd Street. There was a market: vegetables, fruits, meat, poultry. I can still smell the vegetables.

—James Karavolas, who immigrated in 1915 when he was 6

Working in the United States

The jobs that most Greek **immigrants** found required hard, physical work. Some worked in factories making shoes and **textiles.** Others worked on the railroads or in mines. Some sold candy and other items from carts on the street. Many worked as dishwashers or shoe shiners.

This Greek-American family ran a grocery store in the United States. They were photographed in 1932.

This Greek-American man dove for sponges in Tarpon Springs, Florida, in the 1940s. The sponges were sold to people for use in cleaning things.

John Cocoris and his brothers moved from Greece to Tarpon Springs, Florida, in 1905. There, they started a business diving to gather natural sponges in the Gulf of Mexico. They helped hundreds of other Greeks move to Tarpon Springs to work for their company. Tarpon Springs continues to have a large Greek-American population.

The Greek immigrants worked hard and saved money. They usually sent money home to their families in Greece. Many sent money so that family members could buy food. Others sent money so other family members could join them in the U.S.

Business Owners

Upon arriving in the United States, Greek **immigrants** often turned to other Greeks to help them find work. A system called the padrone system came about. The padrone, or boss, would find a job for a worker. Some padrones were not fair. Workers sometimes had to work fifteen hours a day, seven days a week. They also had to pay the padrone a certain amount of the money they made.

Some Greek immigrants came to the U.S. to work in businesses or restaurants that their relatives owned, such as this Greek coffee shop in Aliquippa, Pennsylvania.

This Greek-American man is shown reading a Greek-language newspaper in Pennsylvania in 1941.

The Greek immigrants who got jobs through the padrone system wanted to get out of it quickly. They saved as much money as they could. With the money they saved, Greek immigrants opened restaurants, candy stores, and coffee houses. Other Greek immigrants started Greek-language newspapers. In 1910 there were at least sixteen Greek-language newspapers in the United States.

Coffee houses, or *kafeneion*, were common in Greece. In the United States, they became popular places for Greek-American men to discuss local events.

Later Immigration

In 1924, the United States limited the number of **immigrants** who could come into the country. The number of Greek immigrants did not pick up again until after **World War Two,** when the limit was changed. Between 1946 and 1960, about 56,000 Greeks came to the United States. Many came because their villages had been destroyed during World War Two. They had been left homeless.

Many Greek people came to the U.S. to escape war in their country. These children and adults tried to help people in Greece by asking others to send clothing to Greece.

Some Greek Americans opened restaurants in Greektowns in the U.S. The Parthenon Greek restaurant opened in Chicago in 1968.

There was also a **civil war** between a **communist** group and Greece's government forces. The communist group was defeated in 1949. Some Greeks chose to leave because of the fighting. Like the earlier Greek immigrants, a number of these later immigrants were farmers. But many of the immigrants were not farmers. Some had also gone to college. Others were business owners in Greece. Many of those who came in the second half of the 1900s opened their own businesses in the U.S.

The reason I came to the United States was [because] I was concerned about the education of my kids. Greece in those days had only one university, and if you had kids who wanted to go to the university it was very hard to get the chance.
—George Kokkas, who immigrated in 1967

Customs and Celebrations

Greek Americans have celebrated their **heritage** in the United States since the early 1900s. One important celebration is Greek **Independence** Day on March 25. On this day in 1821, there was a Greek **rebellion** against the **Ottoman Empire.** This led to Greece's **independence** from the Ottoman Empire, which had ruled Greece for 400 years. Greek-American organizations across the United States often put together parades to help remember this day.

These children attended a parade in New York City on Greek Independence Day.

These boys and girls performed a traditional Greek dance at a festival in California.

Cities and towns across the U.S. hold Greek festivals throughout the year. At these festivals, some people wear **traditional** Greek clothes. There is usually traditional Greek music, food, and dancing. The dances that are performed at Greek celebrations come from the different regions, or areas, of Greece. Each region has its own dance.

One Greek dance that is performed at festivals is called the Zorba dance. Dancers stand in a line and hold each other's shoulders. The steps in the dance include many kicks, which start out slowly and then get faster. The dance is performed to a song called "Zorba."

Greek Food

Greek people have introduced many new foods to people in the United States. A gyro is a popular Greek sandwich. It is made with chunks of lamb or beef, tomatoes, onions, and a garlic sauce. All of this is placed on pita bread. Pita bread is a thick, flat bread that is usually round.

Many Greek restaurants serve *saganaki.* This cheese is set on fire before it is served. Everyone yells, "Opa!," which is similar to yelling "Cheers!"

There are many restaurants in the United States that serve Greek food. These people enjoyed a meal of Greek food in Los Angeles, California.

This woman is eating a Greek dessert called baklava. It is made with dough, chopped nuts, honey, and lemon juice.

Shish kebabs are another well-known Greek food. A shish kebab, or souvlakia, includes many items, such as chunks of meats and vegetables, on a long **skewer.** Greeks also brought new cheeses to the U.S. Feta cheese is made from the milk of goats or sheep. It is used in many Greek dishes. Feta cheese is also used in salads.

Arts and Entertainment

Greece has an ancient history. The country is famous for its many great thinkers, **architecture**, and other arts. Greek Americans have continued these **traditions.** Constantino Brumidi **immigrated** to the United States in 1852. He painted the U.S. Capitol building's ceiling and created many other artworks in the building.

Constantino Brumidi, whose father was Greek, said his biggest goal in life was to make the Capitol building beautiful.

Nia Vardalos used stories about her own Greek family in the film My Big Fat Greek Wedding. She wrote the script for the film. A script tells the actors in films the lines they are to say.

Olympia Dukakis grew up in Massachusetts. Her parents were both Greek immigrants. She became an actress and won the Academy Award for her performance in the movie *Moonstruck*.

Several Greek-American performers have become famous over the years. Nia Vardalos grew up in Canada, but moved to the United States to become an actor. She hit it big in Los Angeles when she acted in the film *My Big Fat Greek Wedding*. The movie is about a young Greek-American woman and her family who live in Chicago.

Doctor Kefalides in the U.S.

Nicholas spent ten days in New York City before he moved to Evanston, Illinois, a city near Chicago. He lived there with his aunt and uncle for two years. After finishing his premedical studies, he went to the University of Illinois School of Medicine in Chicago. While in college, Nicholas met a woman named Jane. They fell in love, were married in 1949, and moved into their own home. Nicholas continued working toward his dream of being a doctor.

Nicholas lived with his aunt and uncle in Evanston, Illinois, until he got married. He is shown here with his aunt's nephew and niece, Peter and Nancy.

Nicholas and his wife Jane are shown here with their three children, Patricia, Paul, and Alexandra.

In 1956, that dream came true. After graduating from medical school, Dr. Kefalides continued to work hard. He became a professor of medicine at the University of Pennsylvania. Even though he was studying hard, he still found time to spend with his wife and children. Today, Nicholas and his wife live in Pennsylvania, near Philadelphia. Like many other Greek **immigrants,** Nicholas worked hard to make his dreams come true.

We have passed on our Greek **heritage** through books, annual trips to Greece when the children were young, and to some extent, the Greek church. My wife and I continue to visit Greece every year, and we attend high school class reunions whenever they take place.
　　　　　　　　　　　　　　—Dr. Nicholas Kefalides

Greek Immigration Chart

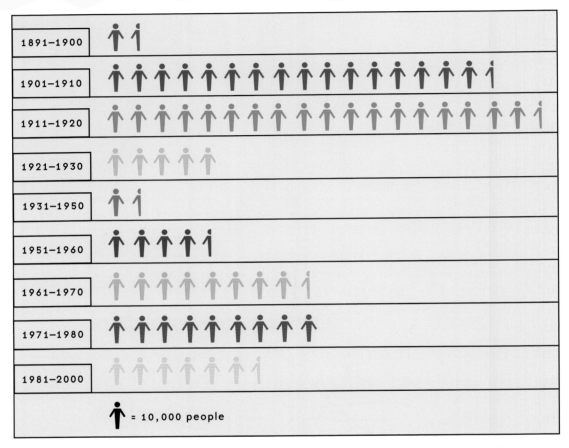

1891–1900	
1901–1910	
1911–1920	
1921–1930	
1931–1950	
1951–1960	
1961–1970	
1971–1980	
1981–2000	

= 10,000 people

*The largest number of Greek **immigrants** moved to the United States in the early 1900s.*

Source: U.S. Immigration and Naturalization Service

More Books to Read

Greene, Meg. *Greek Americans.* San Diego, Calif.: Lucent Books, 2004.

Klingel, Cynthia Fitterer. *Greek Americans.* Chanhassen, Minn.: Child's World, 2003.

Wallner, Rosemary. *Greek Immigrants, 1890–1920.* Mankato, Minn.: Blue Earth Books, 2003.

Glossary

architecture art of designing and creating buildings

civil war war fought between people who live in the same country

communist person or government that supports communism, a political system in which there is one party and government owns all factories, natural resources, and goods

concentration camp camp used during World War Two by the German army to hold anyone who fought against it. People were often killed in concentration camps.

currant tiny raisin

heritage something passed down from one generation to the next

immigrate to come to a country to live there for a long time. A person who immigrates is an immigrant.

independence condition of being free from the rule of other countries, governments, or people

mainland main part of a country's land, as opposed to island parts of a country

Ottoman Empire territories ruled by Turkish leaders. The Ottoman Empire was founded in the 1300s and ruled several lands and people for more than 600 years.

port city near water where ships dock and leave from

quarantine when a sick person is kept in a certain area away from other people so as not to make others sick

rebellion open fight against authority or ruling power

shish kebab dish that includes chunks of meat and vegetables on a skewer

skewer long sharp piece of metal used to cook food over flames

steerage place on a ship where passengers who pay the least to travel stay

textile fabric and material used for making clothing and other items

tradition belief or practice handed down through the years from one generation to the next

World War Two war fought from 1939 to 1945 by Germany, Japan, and Italy on one side and the United States, Great Britain, China, Poland, France, and the Soviet Union on the other

Index